The Lammas Hireling

Ian Duhig worked with homeless people for fifteen years in England and Northern Ireland before becoming a writer and teacher of Creative Writing. He has since held Fellowships at Durham, Lancaster, Leeds and Newcastle Universities. He has won the National Poetry Competition twice, the Forward Tolman Cunard Best Single Poem Prize, an Arts Council Writers' Award and a Cholmondeley Award.

The *Lammas Hireling*

Ian Duhig

PICADOR

First published 2003 by Picador
an imprint of Pan Macmillan Ltd
Pan Macmillan, 20 New Wharf Road, London N1 9RR
Basingstoke and Oxford
Associated companies throughout the world
www.panmacmillan.com

ISBN 0 330 49238 1

9 8 7 6 5 4 3 2 1

A CIP catalogue record for this book is available from
the British Library.

Phototypeset by Intype London Ltd
Printed and bound in Great Britain by
Mackays of Chatham plc, Chatham, Kent

For Peter and Kath

Contents

Acknowledgements

The *Guardian*, *Independent on Sunday*, *Poetry London*, *Poetry Review*, *Near East Review*, 'Eye on the Aire' Newsletter.

'The Lammas Hireling' won the 2001 National Poetry Competition and Forward Tolman Cunard Best Poem Prize, appearing in the 2002 Forward Book of Poetry.

BBC's Poetry Proms commissioned 'There is No Rose of Such Virtue', Cannon Poets 'The Lark in the Clear Air', the Durham Literature Festival 'Brother Robert's Double Vision', Shakespeare's Globe Education 'Vilbia' and the Literature Department of the South Bank Centre 'Midnight on the Water'. 'Rustics Dancing Outside an Inn' was commissioned to accompany a reproduction of the watercolour with that title by Samson Towgood Roche in the Ulster Museum/Abbey Press Anthology *Conversation Piece*, edited by Adrian Rice. 'American Graffiti I & II' were commissioned for the lavatory walls of the Salisbury Arts Centre in 1999 and subsequently appeared in the Picador anthology *Last Words*, edited by Jo Shapcott and Don Paterson.

'Four More Sides to the Franks Casket' was written for W.N. Herbert's web magazine 'The Franks Casket', hosted by the English Department of Newcastle University. 'At Quark's Bar, Deep Space Nine' was written for Iron Press' '*Star Trek*': *The Poems* anthology edited by Valerie Laws.

'Traditional Irish Charm' was written for a session at Southlands School, North Shields, and will appear in the Bloomsbury young persons' anthology *Wicked Poems*, edited by Roger McGough. 'The Viaduct Love Suicide' was written for *The Gift* anthology for the NHS, published by Stride and edited by David Morley. It is dedicated to the women working in the NHS and the memory of Helen Rogan.

Finally, I must thank Northern Arts and the Universities of Durham and Newcastle for the Northern Arts Literary Fellowship, during which much of this book was written.

Ian Duhig

The Lammas Hireling

Blood

Tiptoed to flex your brand new Squire Shop oxblood
  oxfords,
Their Chippendale-varnish palimpsests of spit and polish
Finished with one occult pass from the black shoe-brush
To Rembrandt a veneer even now reflecting veal-pale calves,
White Orlon ankle socks beneath petrol-blue Levi Sta-Prest,
Their baked creases rising to the occasion of red braces,
Clip-ons, a half-inch in width, over brick red and duck egg
Brunswick triple-stripe button-down collared Ben Sherman,
Rizla packet – and packet-of-three-shaped bulges in its
  pocket,
Then up to plenty more 14-year-old slunk-vellum neck,
Bum fluff, stench of Brut, cod and chips, light and bitter,
Pilot-style, gold-framed, honey-tint-lensed Polaroids,
Crop fuzzed from No 2 skin to a chichi revisionist suedehead
Inclined to the painted window of Luke's Tattoo Parlour,
Affecting a genuine temptation to turn over a new leaf
Of your as-yet still-virginal unilluminated manuscript
For a Yakuza bodysuit, blood eagle, bull's head, serpent,
Web, dragon, axe, scrolled heart, skull, drum or trumpet,
Knowing them to be erasable only by Goldfinger's laser
  beam;
Though last Wednesday, outside the school nurse's office,
In front of the whole queue of third years, you blacked out
Just at the glimpse of her lance of a vaccination needle.

The Lammas Hireling

For Robert Walters

After the fair, I'd still a light heart
And a heavy purse, he struck so cheap.
And cattle doted on him: in his time
Mine only dropped heifers, fat as cream.
Yields doubled. I grew fond of company
That knew when to shut up. Then one night,

Disturbed from dreams of my dear late wife,
I hunted down her torn voice to his pale form.
Stock-still in the light from the dark lantern,
Stark naked but for the fox-trap biting his ankle,
I knew him a warlock, a cow with leather horns.
To go into the hare gets you muckle sorrow,

The wisdom runs, muckle care. I levelled
And blew the small hour through his heart.
The moon came out. By its yellow witness
I saw him fur over like a stone mossing.
His lovely head thinned. His top lip gathered.
His eyes rose like bread. I carried him

In a sack that grew lighter at every step
And dropped him from a bridge. There was no
Splash. Now my herd's elf-shot. I don't dream
But spend my nights casting ball from half-crowns
And my days here. Bless me, Father, I have sinned.
It has been an hour since my last confession.

King's Cross, Xmas 2000

The stationmaster moans he's not a prophet:
The Virgin train is going 'at some time'.
No man on earth would blame me if I croaked him,
No court on earth convict me of the crime.

'I wasted time and now doth time waste me';
Some teacher gave me that a thousand times
To train my tender growth in punctual ways
And show he could make punishments fit crimes –

My next late morning, sent to see the Head,
He left venetian blinds where no sun shines.
But now I'm adult, ruler of my life,
Of all that I survey, of all these lines.

Millennia ago this route was brilliant,
Inspiring one cute poem from Tony Harrison
Where new stealth planes and stealthy Viking ships
Are subject to provocative comparison.

I've bought *The Prophecies of Nostradamus*
To see what he might say about my train,
To make what sense I might make of his quatrains,
To try and make connections in my brain.

He saw through time, his editor maintains,
It's just that scrying-water must be muddied;

So DAM means SadDAM (why not NostraDAMus?).
It's little risk predicting we'll get flooded.

Phrases read well: violence 'a false poem',
Or that 'to speak the truth some mouths must close'.
I shifted when I read 'a bovine plague'
Would follow swiftly after waters rose . . .

. . . *'Sur le milieu du grand monde, la rose!'*
He really sounds much better in the French.
His face a mask of empathetic wisdom,
The stationmaster stood behind my bench.

'On the great world's centre, behold the rose!'
As rails grow stations, syntax blooms in speech,
So poetry can knot the rood of words
In ways no university can teach:

A train flies quickly through life's noisy tunnel
Then bursts into eternity again;
Relax before you hurtle at the light –
You can't smell roses when you're on a train!

In this new light I knew I had misthought him,
Ignored the beam in my eye for his mote;
I understood he had a lot to say
And so, from ear to ear, I cut his throat.

There Isn't Why
(Johannes Scheffler)

There isn't why about the rose,
It blooms because that's what it does;
It doesn't care if it gets seen,
It doesn't care what this might mean.

Though flying worms swoop left and right,
The dozy rose snores through the night;
And symbolizing love and lust,
About those too it isn't fussed.

We tell the rose that Christ is born,
It answers slowly with a yawn;
We pin the rose upon the Cross,
And still it doesn't give a toss.

And if its bush should burn with God,
As like as not the rose will nod;
Though round the rose such subjects buzz,
There isn't why about the rose.

Taking My Measure

*Every decided colour does a certain violence to the eye and forces
the organ to opposition* – Goethe, *Theory of Colours*

Bet the last whistle you got fitted for was a 2-Tone Tonik?
Down the Palais giving it brown-gold brown-gold brown . . .
Oh. Funeral. Never mind, sir, I'll do you a second skin, an
Investment – be more of these from now on. Arms out, please.
Read any good books lately, sir? An anthology of German
    poetry?
OK. Not enough English? Oh yes, I've looked at some.
    Novalis?
A depressive mining engineer born during an eclipse of the
    sun,
His first and only love Sophie croaking before he could wurst
    her,
Of course he wrote hymns to the night and died of
    consumption,
That little black dress on every rack of sexy fatal illnesses,
A classic standby fall-back and drop-dead gorgeous
    accessorized
With a skimmed-milk-blue corsage and pre-existentialist
    bullshit
To set off the neo-Counter-Reformation revanchist
    thanatolatry –
'Unscorchable stands the Cross, victory banner of our faith!'
Did I mention that 'cretin' is French for 'Christian', sir?

I know for alchemists like him the Cross meant light, *ros crux*,
The dew cross, gold's solvent – we get all that old bollocks
Down the lodge. No one believes it. It's an excuse to get pissed
Like Rilke's alchemist – and Rilke? Done in by a poxy rose?
Want me to sew in a cosh-pocket in case you're jumped by
    tulips?
Just having a laugh, sir, just having a laugh. So what side do
You dress on, sir, or isn't that an issue for you any more?

A Dream of Wearing String Vests Forever
For Brendan Kennelly

For everything that lives
Is holy. For a string vest
Does more than only connect;
Embodying kinship networks,

It is my ancestral tartan,
 – 'The Breakfasting Duhig' –
Light as an aura massage
Or love's gappy language.

An ontological conundrum:
Nothingness-patched being!
What is the length of a piece?
To what lengths will it go?

Only so far; it can't flatter.
But a must in emigrants' kit:
Though born in Antarctica,
It's as at home in Africa.

And if a gaffe at the opera,
It's a good sign in hosts,
Of ease with their guests.
It grows like the universe,

Constantly, in every direction;
A dreamcatcher however stretched
Holding its integrity and warmth.
Dad's gift. To get the hang of it.

The Lark in the Clear Air

For Chrissie Glazebrook

All dewy-eyed, my sister told me how
She once got up before the dawn to see
Her birthday rising on the Glen of Aherlow.
She skipped up frosty fields like bleaching sheets
But heading back, she paused to catch her breath,
And saw her footprints spread out everywhere
Like ginger biscuits on a tablecloth.
She gently hummed *The Lark in the Clear Air*,
Judged her run-up to some cooling cow-shit,
Guessed when its crust would be Mass-wafer-thin
Then took off, flew and landed slap-bang in it,
To feel the quick give of that eggshell skin
Then buinneach surging hot between her toes.
'Tomorrow she shall', as her old song goes.

Chinese Sonnets

I

Pursuing eternal life,
Qin, the first Chinese emperor,
Sent ships with crews of children
To find the Islands of the Blest
And return with their secrets.
When he returned to his palace,
Dead fish escorted his train
To cloak his noble corpse's stench.

II

Our Oxherd constellation
(Three close stars in your Aquila)
And that one, Weaving Maiden
(Vega, with Lyra for her loom),
Watch each other, full of love,
Either side of the Milky Way,
That great river of the night,
Like Running Bear, Little White Dove.

III

When I told my son of Yu,
Born by Caesarean section
On the corpse of his father,
And of the virgins made pregnant
From stepping in God's footprints
Or from eating a swallow's egg,
He said, 'Father, in past times,
Weren't there any natural births?'

Lotus Root Porridge

She breakfasts on lotus root porridge and persimmons
But suffers a dish of reheated chrysanthemum tea,
All the palace wells being poisoned by the corpses
Of her attendant ladies taking the honourable course.

Her son gnaws his sleeve like a silkworm a mulberry leaf,
Or sketches dragons on the deck of the marble gondola
Floated by the whole of last year's budget for the Navy.
He wastes vermilion needed for the Instrument of Surrender.

Collecting eggs from the high rain trees, I saw outside
Her boxers confront a Maxim with their immortal postures.
I clip the wings of all palace birds except for pigeons,
And fix their tails with whistles that sound in flight.

Concrete Poetry

1. Water
(Kurt Bartsch)

The humanist, in the building's charred remains,
With ash for ink, his finger for a pen,
Solemnly traced out 'NEVER AGAIN'.
If only on the first flames
This good humanist
Had pissed!

2. Sand
(Nina Cassian)

My hands tore off across the Whitby sand.
Where, I wondered, were they heading?
Some island of beckoning palms?

And what about my wrists, for all the world
Like Whitby's civic coat of arms,
Two snakes beheaded by St Hild?

3. Cement
(Leopold Staff)

Found your house on solid rock,
You might break your family's back.

Build your house upon the sand,
Then at least they'll know their ground

But hang it on their chimney-smoke:
That's the brickie's masterstroke.

Northumbrian Graffiti

'Behold me now /And my face to a wall',
Writes Hyde translating *Mise Raifteirí*;
'Behold me now /And my back to a wall',
Are the same lines rendered by Stephens.

It is the metaphor of emperors and poets:
The sage we know in Latin as Confucius
Wrote that a man who is ignorant of poetry
Is standing with his face against a wall.

Yet, knock through into Raifteirí's stanza,
You find he doesn't mention walls, but Balla,
The Mayo townland where his poem happened,
As this one's happening here, in Wallsend.

And anyway, the poem isn't Raifteirí's
But by Ó Ceallaigh, or as we'd say, O'Kelly,
Who wrote the famous autobiographical poem
Known in English as 'I Am Raftery'. Behold me now.

American Graffiti I

Women's Room

I open for you my mouth. I open for you
My two eyes, the white chamber of my skull:
From my old tongue, your sentences will rise
For I am Goddess Tlaelquani, Eater of Excrement,
Sister of Tlazoltéotl. Problems with some male?
I cut off his eggs with my obsidian glass knife.
Perhaps an office colleague is harassing you?
I gut him and stuff the corpse with chocolate.
You suspect a carpenter is overcharging you?
I sacrifice his firstborn to the Plumed Serpent.
See? I do have a knack for this sort of thing
And you worship me even by sitting here,
Considering the compact, adjusting the mask.
My mouth must soon close. Open your mouth. Ask.

American Graffiti II

Men's Room

Your look flickers across disinfected surfaces,
Starting at all eye-contact as if it burned
For this is the time and temple of reflection,
Of I, Tlaelquani's sister, great Tlazoltéotl,
Goddess of the skeletons in all your closets.
Should I lick the half-moon of my thumbnail,
Your manhood's index weeps itself to death
Like candlewax running down a feast-day skull.
It is my power and my pleasure to illuminate
Everything you think you've got away with,
The footprints of liars where they first fell:
Your doom burns back up them like a slow fuse
And you won't save yourself by pissing on your shoes.

Salvages

Seemely inough of visage & whyle kempte yet not vaine,
Thei goe in no whispering sylkes but a rattel of flakkes;
No velvette slyppres but workmanlie cattel-skynne shoos.
Theyr howses are comelie. On woden beddes thei dreme
  much.

Yet I spake there amongst scholars ne better than ribalds,
Who mette Word of Jesu with al countrefeicte philosophie,
As 'Man cannot make an worme but turns out goddes in
  batches!'
As 'To compas ease of governaunce is to façion paradys.'

I beleeve theyr elderes are fedde up & despatched at feestes
Or poudred for store as our gammondes & pesteles of
  porkke,
As yffe we are best sepulchred in our chylderne's bowelles.
Theyr skylle at armes is lytel. Theyr mowntaynes blede
  golde.

Meet The Duhigs

Googling, I find on the Duhig genealogical sites
There graze only the most immaculately white sheep,
So we get daguerreotypes of the dashing Union captain –
Not the Private colour-bearer for the Confederates;
Sir James, the longest-serving Archbishop of Brisbane,
Not Cornelius transported on the First Convict Fleet;
Neither Indian Mutiny Medallists nor East End Pat,
Mosley's man, who brought the dockers out for Enoch.

Peggy Cullen traced us back to soupers in the Famine,
Who sold their Catholicism for a mess of pottage, sick
From eating grass. They'd know that in our fathers' house
Are many mansions, with some rooms occupied by doctors
And some by devils, and every key will open every door.

Canon

Barrel.
Shot fish.

At Quark's Bar, Deep Space Nine

My maker took your fascists' cartoon-Jew,
Scaled back its nose but gave me ears like clams
So I won't take abuse, old chap, from you,
Cocksure from pornographic holograms.
Consider an off-camera position:
You called me Shylock when I brought your bill;
I've read outside the Rules of Acquisition
And never bought this worship of your Will –
The 'many-coloured life' he gave each part?
Did that include his Jewish moneylender?
He makes the bar bill read like Jean-Paul Sartre.
You're new, so I don't write you off, big spender,
But I keep tabs and bills and records straight.
Now pay. I'm not here just to educate.

Cutler's Poetry

Whose posy was for all the world like cutler's poetry
upon a knife.
Merchant of Venice, Act V scene i

I was a Soho nightclub doorman,
Which doesn't make me Martin Bormann:
You don't stop fights by tuneful humming
And most I brittled had it coming.
But then one night I learned a lesson,
By courtesy of Smith & Wesson:
I'd stroked this bloke across his hooter
When, bless my soul, he pulls a shooter –
Both it and him went off half-cock
And I cabbaged him, but I'd had a shock.
Soon half our punters packed a gun.
The dance-floor grew more like Verdun:
Chuck someone out for too much booze, he
Comes back blazing with an Uzi.
I'd recently become a father
And getting earache from the carver,
I changed careers to quell her qualms
And started selling antique arms,
With short-term rentals on the side –
For real solutions, nothing schnide!
You'll stabilize your twitching bottle
With a sundang or a shotel,
Though if a sanded-down schiavona

Lends some panache to your chiv owner,
A connoisseur of cold steel stabs
His victims with a honed pesh kabz,
Parang, panja or baselard,
A falchion, a Khyber kard –
Or if he's aiming at your back,
He might select a fine bagh-nakh,
An estoc, Saxon miner's axe,
An aikichu, a scramasax –
A shashqa or a scian dhu
Are ladies' size and damn good too.
So show your mettle at the disco:
This blade's inlaid by Francisco,
The chasing on its bronze ricasso
Calls to mind the late Picasso,
Its Gottfried Pappenheimer hilt
Will help you through survivor guilt,
So cut a dash, don't look borassic,
Slash with an established classic!
See, even laws subscribe to fashion –
The press might stir the public's passion
And if the Filth are told to step on
Possessing an Offensive Weapon,
With my stock you'll have no fears:
All older than one hundred years
And each a certified antique,
The Filth can't do a thing but deek

While if you're found with any gun
You're done and dusted, my old son!
The doors revolve: you go in rich
But come out as some wing king's bitch:
If you don't like it up the arse
Then shop with me and show your class.

Mi Ley

Pizarro cut a notch from the gallows we'd been forced to raise
And said this proved he owned us, and our souls were saved.
I read the words cut in the blood-groove of his sword blade,
Por mi rey es mi ley, meaning, 'for my king this is my law'.

From years in the mines my brother's head would be a riddle,
How even when he stopped breathing it still droned softly.
In sympathy, this poisoned lowland air is mining through my
    face
Where I now harvest swampland coca for my king, this is my
    law.

I remember our true King pushing thorns through his penis,
Blood catching paper from which we priests read prophecies;
Now I see visions of a dragon-pale boy pushing a glass thorn
Into his penis, his last vein. For my King, this is my law.

Ken's Videos, Seahouses

Love and hate are horns on the same goat –
Wise Woman, *The Vikings*

In two minds about renting *The Vikings* from Ken's Videos,
I ask Ken. He shrugs. Acknowledging the cinematography –
'Scorsese adored Cardiff's work' – Ken feels Northumbria,
Like Scorsese's *Raging Bull*, cries out for black and white.

I see again my brother's whole prison wing, a moving barcode
In the black-and-white striped shirts of Newcastle United,
Or away strip washdays. He'd scored his fingers LOVE and
    HATE
To look hard; my soft knight who chased dragons in tin foil.

Ken's voice breaks in to press the case for a recent *Beowulf*:
The baddies, a tribe of matriarchal subhuman cannibals;
The hero, an exiled Arab poet played by Antonio Banderas.
The line grows. On the horns of a helmet, I hesitate, lost.

DXCVII

Romantic histories of England's Christian conversion
Begin with the future Pope Gregory at a slave market,
Stunned into punning by a vision of angelic Angles

And instantly deciding to evangelize their people.
But you must know even then your distant archipelago
Boasted Saints, some still recognized in our Calendar.

And why was a good man consorting with slave traders?
It was the rumours they trafficked which concerned him.
The young slaves he bought were trained as interpreters

And spies. As Pope, he sent them to investigate your Church.
Their first reports were enough to confirm his worst fears.
One name kept cropping up, Colum Cille – to us Columba,

Rogue dove. With landfall on his Iona heart of darkness,
He banned cattle, explaining, 'Where there is a cow,
There will be a woman.' His authority can be assessed

From the years he then spent exorcizing possessed milk,
Divining the whereabouts of fugitive milk-skins and pails,
Proving the local sorcerer's 'bull's milk' was really blood

Or counselling wives to endure the lusts of ugly husbands.
A nudist, a quondam warrior and convicted psalter-thief,
Against his invention of a vegetarian and pacifist knife

We must set that magic trapper's stake he gave some beggar
On which fish, flesh and fowl impaled themselves constantly.
Doctrinally, he was suspect, evidenced by his *Song of Trust*:

'I do not adore the voice of birds, nor sneezing, nor lots,
Nor a boy, nor women; my druid is Christ . . .' Sneezing?
One of our men wormed his way into Columba's inner circle,

Learning where the bodies were buried. Literally –
Like Odhran's, the human sacrifice who was built alive
Into the foundations of the first church raised on Iona.

For Pope Gregory this was enough. In that year of Our Lord,
Columba would die on Iona and Augustine land in Kent.
You believe in God: do you think this could be an accident?

Vilbia

Qui mihi Vilbiam involavit sic liquat como do aqua –
Curse-tablet found in Bath:
'May he who carried off Vilbia from me become as liquid as water'.

I

He got to where he'd say he's come to love me,
When suddenly, mid-lie, he stalled above me –
Thinning like air great heat was making shiver,
He held a second, a bridge of glass,
Realized the horror coming to pass,
Then pissed himself from ice to raging river,
Breaking on me in some undoing birth
That pulled him back inside his mother earth.

II

I put on a clean robe. I spoke a prayer.
Then I washed that man right out of my hair.

Four More Sides to the Franks Casket

A POEM FOR THE NET

Fastitocalon's Congregation

More island than beast, sailors call
This creature Fastitocalon the Whale.
If hungry, he need but yawn to lace
A sea for miles with scented trails:
Shining schools drawn to their source
Pack Fastitocalon's enormous mouth
Like a cinema, until his huge jaw rises,
A cruel curtain, and the lights go down.

Revision

Up the whale-road to the coast of the Danes
Sailed Urv, Ing historian. Leder his hosen,
His armband scarlet, centre-crossed with runes
For rebirth and oxen. He barked in their streets:
'Hark to me, Vikings! Heed me, blood brothers!
In Vinland they're filming slights on your past,
On gentle St Grendel – worse on his Mother,
The Baltic Madonna, Our Lady of Danes!'

The Abbess Sees Her Physician

You don't impress me with your strings of Latin:
Tacitus thought all English pearls the colour
Of navel fluff, while Bede lists violet, green,
Berry-red, Byzantine-silk purple – on my neck,
I'll flaunt these tumours you're so keen to cure.
I set new budgets with the pig bishop tomorrow.
Watch their effect on him. The rise will buy books
You've leeched on at me for months to order.

Legend

A beached King of Terror
Yielded his cage of bones
For this ark of dark scrimshaw,
But know too from these runes,
Warned by Our Lady's Prophet,
He'll come back with attitude
To land the world in his net
Of longitude and latitude.

Wise, Brave Old Njal

Across the Althing, the two families fence:
Flosi cuts Njal's eldest with 'shitbeard';
He ripostes that Flosi is 'a troll's bitch'.
Seeing the warriors rush off for weapons,

Njal declares the meeting adjourned *sine die*.
Vikings together are like the dry chickweed
That Flosi's men will collect for kindling
When they torch Njal's mansion on their raid.

Offered escape by Flosi, Njal will refuse,
Nobly, so his burning serve as firebreak
In the obligations of their family feud.
His chosen weapon was the pointed saying:

'The arm's joy in the blow is brief';
'Seines may miss where purse nets catch';
'Birds land on ears of wheat not spears'.
If I was with them I'd have lent a match.

Brother Robert's Double Vision

'To such a pitch of folly I am brought,
Being caught between the pull
Of the dark moon and the full'
Yeats, 'The Double Vision of Michael Robartes'

In Bede's *Historia Ecclesiastica Gentis Anglorum*,
I pause at Gregory's judgement on Augustine's question
As to whether it's sinful to take the Body of Christ
After suffering what he terms 'dream-like illusions.'
These might be dyspepsia, Gregory confidently writes,
So they should bar no one from the Blessed Sacrifice.

On Lindisfarne last Easter I lost my appetite at the stone
Marking where the Norsemen preyed on our brothers first:
It moved me to offer up psalms for them on my way home.
I chose to follow the same path as that miraculous ox
That led the monks with Cuthbert's uncorrupted corpse
To found our most Christian city, our beloved Durham.

Yet on a journey I know well, I found myself lost.
Still singing at midnight, supperless, unstarlit,
Something struck me with all the force of revelation:
I woke with no shoes and a song in my sore head;
'If hosen or shoon thou have never given nane
So the fire shall eat through thee to thy bare bane.'

I comforted myself recalling how the wild druids
Would get inside an ox-skin to see the future –
I'd be more Christian barefoot. At my Foundation,
I couldn't settle. My Confessor suggests interpretations
But I quibble. Even beef no longer agrees with me.
Worried by certain texts, I worry them continually:

Eriugena's *Scripture and Nature: The Shoes of Christ*,
Alcuin blaming the King for the Lindisfarne raid,
'Woe to you who sold the poor for a pair of shoes!'
In a library that might have shod ten thousand.
Last night I must have bolted my ale, for I dreamt
Of our gospel-pages nailed out, becoming drumheads.

Died for Love
(The Galla of Ethiopia)

Were I a fine ox, I'd buck off my yoke:
My owner would beat me until his stick broke;
He'd cut more sticks and beat more and after I died,
He'd butcher my body and auction my hide.

Beautiful women will want one so fine,
But She will pay double, then She will be mine;
She'll smuggle me home with no word to her kin
And rub rich oils into my tenderized skin;

She'll hold me and mould me – relaxed, I'll grow longer,
Drunk as our incenses warm and grow stronger;
Wrapped up in each other from midnight through noon,
Our sanctuary candles, the sun and the moon;

Her husband will shout as his house rolls and rocks,
'Get off that smelly old skin of an ox!'
But we'll stay together, as close in our love
As foot to sandal, as hand to glove.

Golden Lotus

The poet fell in love with me, he wrote,
Catching my reflection in the Dragon Pool
At the Three Religions Temple on Pig Day.
My first Ceremony of the Crescent Moons,

They touched my arches with a writing brush
For pointedness on the Sevenfold Standard –
More than four inches, the lotus is only silver.
Our golden poet thinks my cunt is tight

Because of how the golden lotus makes us walk.
I haven't walked a step in fifteen years.
Sometimes he eats almonds from between my toes.
Sometimes he fucks the cleft in my left foot.

'The Vision of the Virgin'

For his climactic Divine Comic strip
Illustrating Dante's *Paradiso*
Botticelli wrote this title, then stopped
And left the vellum blank. It was as though

There is No Rose of Such Virtue

Our Lady of Atheists, broken from hope,
I prayed to You; somehow that helped me cope.
Mad shot in the dark. Much like my verse.
But all that white night, bad didn't turn worse.

I ask for a young man with rings round his eyes,
No stock to take care of, he struggles to rise
Till night yields to night with hardly a seam –
Asleep or awake, it replays like a dream:

The needles of truth in the haystacks of crap,
The watching slow death creep over the map,
The tact and compassion the bureaucrat wields,
The speedwell and silence that strangle his fields.

His wife's hell's his talk. It goes round and round.
All flesh is brass. They sold out the pound.
When all's said and done what was done was what spun.
She waters his whisky. She's buried his gun.

The sun or the moon is over Great Mell.
Some Canada geese are scouting the fell.
It's Beltane so increase is honoured with fire.
The trumpet of smoke slowly lifts itself higher.

Last Star in the Darkness, Shot Silk of the Kine;
There's other madonnas but You are all mine.
Our Lady of Atheists, I know You're not there.
That doesn't matter. Answer my prayer.

Glass Talk

She used such words as 'whimsey', 'ponty', 'cullet' ... and it
intrigued Mr Carpenter. Never had he met a woman who could
talk glass before.
The Glass Virgin, Catherine Cookson

With the last rack forked into the annealing kilns,
The time freed before the next contracted stint
Was spent on exhibition pieces or Christmas gifts:
The blowing irons became their own trumpets, raising

Poems from flint glass, a tall ship cast in water,
A bird from air, articulating rosary beads, all
Gathered and spun and tweaked from the fizzing light
And borax and cullet, then nursed at the glory-hole

As Catherine worshipped at the furnace of the word
But drew back from poetry, her first true romance,
Beating out the fluent rainbow of her paraison to prose's
Transparent panes, trimmed, squared off, filling shelves

As she bought libraries for the local university
To honour her with a calculatedly second-rank degree;
She who sent me questing for what poets most love,
To find the meanings of words, of words like 'graal'.

SS-Unterscharführer Otto Rahn of the Dachau Research Unit Lectures at the Dietrich Eckart Society, Düsseldorf, 9/1/1938

Thank you, Cultural Secretary Eggars, for that most generous introduction; and my thanks also to Dr Heinrichsdorff, who will be covering my talk this evening for *The Westphalia Gazette*. It is a deep pleasure for me as a patriot and a poet to be asked to address this august body named for that paragon poet–patriot and dedicatee of *My Struggle*. An aptness too, perhaps, in that my subject should be the Cathars, whose faith claimed most of the Provençal troubadours. Indeed it was another poet, Dante, who first named their region for its distinctive pronunciation of the word yes, '*lingua d'Oco*'. Cathars, whose own name derives from the Greek root of 'pure', deemed this whole, visible world of ours as delusional. They called it 'the Devil's clothes', a conspiracy woven of 'gold and fields, vineyards, silver and wives' while they believed that Christ of His own nature could not be mechanically born but was in their image 'shadowed' in Mary, not of actual Jewish flesh Himself. Cathars led decent, frugal lives on which were visited Dantean torments because of the ambitions of the Pope in Rome and the King in Paris. Imagine, if you will, a hundred naked men in single file, each's hands on the shoulders of his brother in front, stumbling through the April countryside of Southern France, to which they pay as little heed as they do to the dazzling sunshine. Crusaders blinded ninety-nine, leaving their first man one eye alone to guide this vision of Christian mildness back to Carcassonne. Our faith too was persecuted; we too suffered martyrdom. We symbolize this in our most sacred relic, the Blood Flag. I begin therefore with an examination of the view that the most sacred relic of the Cathars, the Holy Grail, had only a poetic existence – was in fact a linguistic figure, a pun, such as Christ was given to, in this case from an Old Romance dialect, on 'San Greal' and 'Sang Real', where 'Sang' means 'blood', leading us to the consideration that this refers to an identifiable inherited factor. I have found no empirical evidence for this among my sample groups. A glass of water, please.

'I Butcher for the Wehrmacht Catering Corps'

For Irina Gavrilchenko

I butcher for the Wehrmacht Catering Corps,
Kharkov slave labour in the Patriotic War,
And sometimes I steal cows' blood in a bottle
Because it fries up like a purple omelette.

We sold Fabergé Eggs for our Five Year Plans,
I handled the red one ribbed with diamonds –
Inside, a yellow rosebud in the German taste
To comfort Alexandra, our homesick Tsarina.

My mother in the kitchen boiled yellow eggs red
With berries for our sins and the blood Christ shed,
Then we broke them with nails to signify
Our pure new souls from His sacrifice;

My grandmother sang about hares laying eggs
Like the song I heard about Sniper Zaitsev,
His name means 'hare', his squad's called *leverets*
And their egg-timer sights fill with yellow heads.

I butcher for the Wehrmacht Catering Corps,
Kharkov slave labour in the Patriotic War,
And sometimes I steal cows' blood in a bottle
Because it fries up like a purple omelette.

Rustics Dancing Outside an Inn
For Elio Cruz

Scorpions rule the sand once Babylon; a spider binds
Kubla's bones; God is dead; the French are on the sea;
And in his whitewashed Bath atelier Samson Towgood
   Roche

Finishes the picture and his picture inside the picture
Commissioned to the title *Rustics Dancing Outside an Inn*
(A tight blue jacket bellowing Jolly. Got that? Jolly.)

He steps back. No one will really look at it anyway.
They'll glimpse a new daub hanging over the damp patch.
But there's more in it Samson knew they'd think worth
   hanging:

In middle distance, a neurasthenic Anglican cathedral
Steams through the gathering waves of the countryside.
Edging round one corner of the Spa Inn, a liberty tree

Menaces some baked hedgehogs cooling on the porch roof.
Hope and Charity are mob-capped concierges at the door:
At the window, Faith is over a barrel. Chickens fly home.

Right, her bustle the size and shape of mainland China,
A nurse ignores her charge's hand become a scorpion's claw.
Beyond them, a tight blue jacket is pouring Death a double

Cream. Soon they'll reel about like cows. Opposite:
The dancing couple. He's as smug as buttered parsnips
Despite entertaining scarlatina and an eerie crotch.

Clearly, he fancies himself a Burke to her Marie Antoinette.
She seems brightness of brightness, her brow without flaw,
But look closer: there is no sense of freedom in her steps.

Consider too the blood-red rosebud mouth, breast implants
And bound feet. But the sand in her hourglass figure is set
To burst its stay and utter forth scorpions upon this city

Awash with watery men of watery taste drinking watery tea,
This waste of pastel stucco, this snotty Godforsaken Bath!
Samson Towgood Roche laughs to himself, silently, for ever.

Water, Light

The swerving Aire would take as fair
Cows Celts killed to give her:
What crimes were these to BCC's
Which took the entire river?

In mining by the ox-bow lake
They breached the navigation
And twenty million tons of river
Changed its destination;

They flooded opencast and pit
And turned the site to sludge,
Likewise the hopes of management
Of selling it to Budge.

Some people couldn't run a bath
And these were running mining;
Bloodied, bowed but round their cloud
There shone our silver lining:

Lost boats from St Aidan's past
Were relaunched from the dead
Now local archaeologists
Could dig Aire's river bed.

These craft that took the air again
Were often Viking-sailed,
And seen beside their brilliant pride
The dingy dinghy paled.

Like eagles' wings their ribs spread wide,
Between them, in the green,
They made a find: a coin that shined!
Aire water burned it clean –

Eric Houlder told us this,
It's not me having laughs:
Untreated water from the Aire
Developed photographs.

In my mind's darkroom one clears now,
Time's misty lens is wiped;
With raiders then it wasn't sails
But suits that would be striped.

To raise their sale, the BCC
Gave Budge more than they ought to;
He bought their mud and sold their flood
To drought-struck Yorkshire Water.

So where's St Aidan's other boats?
Your question's bang to rights:
No power station runs on air,
You burned them in your lights.

Coble Rig Veda

Found Poem, (from *A Seahouses Saga*,
A. C. Rutter)

The rig was simplicity itself,
Lending itself to swift handling.
The jib tack cringle would be bent
On the bowsprit and shoved outboards

Through the gammon, the single rope
Halliard fast to the peak cringle
Ready for hoisting, the sheet laid
Handy to the foot of the mast.

The mainsail, a dipping lug laid along
What would be the lee side with the half-
Ring in the yard hooked into the traveller.
There was a single block halliard tied

Loosely on the weather belaying pin,
With the tack cringle hooked to the
Gun tackle down-haul on the weather
Shoulder and all was set.

Midnight on the Water

I

Assassinated by the sky,
From Lorca's 'Poet in New York';
The ripples from that line
Keep pulling me back.

Like the poor trudged their labyrinths
Under cathedral rose windows
On virtual pilgrimages,
My words circled Ground Zero.

Every cripple finds a way to walk,
Was one of my father's kindly phrases;
His foot was often in his mouth,
His heart usually in the right place.

A dream of my childhood Hero Twins:
In my uncle's gunshop in New York,
My father, in his Irish Army uniform.
Even here they refuse to talk.

Cod Nostradamus from the net:
Great thunder in the City of God;
The Two Brothers torn apart by Chaos!
Dated when he was a century dead.

A 'Northern Echo' processing error
To its own website invents
The requiem for every faith:
   ... *a thousand-word silence.*

II

The collection's silent at the benefit concert
For the New York Firemen at the Miners' Hall.
The singer's voice is an uncut diamond;
On some notes, you hear the coal:

Let's think of Mrs Burnett,
Once had sons but now has none;
By the Trimdon Grange Explosion,
Joseph, George and James are gone.

Lost brothers, lost battles,
Assassinated Lorca;
The last song the band plays
Is *Midnight on the Water.*

My train back's so late
I see out the night
And the stars on the windows
Extinguished with light.

[55]

My head rings with lines
From poems and a song:
The labyrinths of crosses,
Our time is not long;

Give a beer to the fiddler,
The rule of the corn;
A thousand glass tambourines
Wounding the dawn.

The Stake

Penny a poppy!
Its petals, she said,
Would cover the stains
On Herbert's chest.

She bought two poppies:
Their little black eyes,
She said, were opened
By Herbert's trial.

She bought three poppies,
For she said their stems
Were green as that squad
Of trembling men.

She bought four poppies;
Their pins were a steel,
She said, that was softer
Than what she feels.

She bought five poppies
And rattled a tin,
So for her shilling
I remember him:

Private Herbert Burden,
Northumberland Fusiliers,
Born 1899, Volunteered 1914,
Shot at dawn, 20th July 1917.

The Fiddle Teacher

For G.N.

When Padraig played one lullaby,
The big old door key in his teeth,
He'd stroke it on his fiddle's bridge
To raise a teething baby's cry.

She puts new keys between their teeth
And cuts them on the great and gone;
She breaks the silences they clutch
To wake the fiddlers underneath.

Sí

I keep the usual string of nightmares: fires, falling,
My feet earthfast while the unseen horror closes in –
But also some good bloodstock. This is a favourite:
To start, echoey children's chanting in my father's
Tipperary accent, 'Are you a witch or are you a fairy,
Or are you the wife of Michael Cleary?' I know both,

Cooper Michael, dressmaker Bridget; childless, envied.
One day she ails, won't mend. Changed, the wise man says.
The doctor is whiskey-cheerful. 'Stroke,' Michael repeats,
Like *poc sí*, a fairy stroke. Only water breaks her fast.
She can't be made to answer her name three times over,
Nor has blood enough to sign it once, the wise man says.

After the last rites, the priest eats eggs and boxty.
Michael returns from Fethard with nine cures of herbs,
Boiling them in the first milk given after a calving.
The wise man has to hold her down. She spews it up.
So Michael douses the changeling in burning lamp oil
To free his real wife from Kylenagranagh fairy fort.

There the R.I.C. find him nursing a black-hafted knife.
Still now the cold moon of his heart eclipses my own,
Till like a circus animal jumping through a paper hoop,
A white horse from the fairy fort bursts through my chest
In showers of ash, bone splintered like bits of teeth,
And a beautiful screaming woman is tied to its saddle.

Romance of the Cuckolded Hunter

(Spanish Anonymous)

'Cold, ill-shod, my nails jammed with hog's blood,
Seven long days have I hunted this valley:
Drive on, my dogs, forwards or die of distempers –
Boar killed on Thursday is yours for the Friday!'

'A long seven years have I fought in this breastplate;
Sun-bright Lady, might I rest my head here tonight?'
'You're welcome to sleep, sir, disarm and be fearless,
Tie your horse in the courtyard, coal-black knight.'

'Dogs tempt me no longer from the Emperor's daughter;
Welcome me, wife, I walk in the orchard!'
From where she lay softly in the Moor's embrace,
She heard him shout. Hard tears burned her face.

'Who owns that horse with its airs above the ground?'
'For your love of warfare, a gift from my father.'
'Whose is that lance, with its watersilk blade?'
'For your love of the chase, a gift from my brother.'

'Whose gift old armour? Whose gift a crescent sword?'
She unsheathed the sword and struck off his head;
Her hair flew about her like branches round an oak
And the silk of her veil shivered with her stroke.

The Officer of the Jewish Watch
(de la Berceo)

The Jewish watch posted to Jesus's tomb were drunken
    smart alecs
Who mocked believers in His Godhead with ugly figs of
    music
Tortured from cheap fiddles and zithers, knee-harps and
    rebecs.

Then their officer spoke: 'When names are named and faces
    framed
For this death, men, it strikes me that it would be a crying
    shame
If the Romans as a whole people were to end up getting
    blamed.'

Fortunes

(Anglo-Saxon)

Watching children play, we know
They're bought with grace from night,
To show them what we hope is love
And the world's turning light.

Soon we're paying out their growth
In clothes and shoes and caps,
But what's in store for them in turn?
That girl who's 'tig' perhaps.

See her a woman wiping her footprints
From the dewfall's silver memory;
She bears a child and injuries,
Wife to Jew, Gypsy, refugee.

This child here will betray his lord
And be crucified on the crossroads tree –
Hear him cry then, his wits astray.
His playmates burn out his family.

That one drowns. Those grow rich.
She, with twelve's endeavour –
See her shin up an apple tree.
She must fall. She falls for ever.

More than Cain's clan bear a mark:
That laughing boy? Grief will break him.
The night is strong, our roads dark,
Christ the way. Take him.

Traditional Irish Charm

For All at Southlands School,
North Shields

Buinneach buí
Bliaina ort
Agus é chomh ag tanaí
Le blathach.

I curse you to suffer with
Projectile diarrhoea
As runny as buttermilk
For one entire year.

Rosary

I.M.

All Billy Shiel's boats are called 'Glad Tidings'.
The last will ferry me across to Andrew Waterhouse
Where he is writing now, with an upside-down coble
For his home and office on his own unnoticed Farne.

There, terns' eggs litter stones that are also eggs
Under the millennium party of the Northern Lights.
They'll show me the way to find Andrew, waiting for me.
He'll tell me again what he told me in the Bridge Hotel,

How the individual pages of the Lindisfarne Gospels,
If left too near a fire, shrink from it, and start
To reassume the shapes of the calves they parted from
And I know if I ask, he'll tell me all their names.

Beadnell Sands

'A lady like you should take special care round here,
Where midwives clip between the toes of most newborn.
A seal is a double beast, fish nor flesh, silkie, selkie,
Sneaking among kine for milk. I have found things hidden

Under hedgerows in cornfields, black christening gowns
Made from God knows what. Husbands are forsaken
While they sing to receive the souls of new suicides,
Pods of scent and shadows left behind in their places.

Here. Let me walk you home.' With that he turned inland,
But slurred his feet, turned back again and all he saw
Was Beadnell's printless sand put on the sea, and the tears
He shed were seven, and the cries he raised were three.

The Viaduct Love Suicide

'*Farewell the world,*
Farewell to the night';
Farewell my family,
Forgive me this flight.

I did my husband's
Though with him was gone
The last of the good times
For me and our son.

When I needed bread
Life gave me stones;
That fairy-tale giant
Made bread from my bones.

Hard our communion,
A stone for a host:
My son, you are special,
Different from most,

And most take against
The different as strange;
With names if not stones
They take their revenge.

The first two lines of this poem are from Chikamatsu's
'The Sonezaki Love Suicide'.

We're turning to air
That no stone can touch.
You made my life, son,
I love you so much.'

She stepped from the bridge
Her child in her arms
To join with the earth
No providence harms.

Wind from the wheatfields
Blows through Bridgehill
The last light of evening
Falls on Blackhill

It falls still on Consett
And Leadgate and Delves.
This song is over.
Look after yourselves.